Love's

Motive

Love's Motive

Ben Fisher

Why Publishing

Copyright © 2021 by Ben Fisher

All rights reserved. No part of this book may be reproduced in any manner whatsoever without written permission except in the case of brief quotations embodied in critical articles and reviews.

First Printing, 2021

ISBN: 978-1-8383531-6-2

Unless otherwise stated, Scripture quotations are from the ESV® Bible (The Holy Bible, English Standard Version®), copyright © 2001 by Crossway, a publishing ministry of Good News Publishers. Used by permission. All rights reserved.

Scripture quotations [marked NIV] taken from the Holy Bible, New International Version Anglicised Copyright © 1979, 1984, 2011 Biblica

Used by permission of Hodder & Stoughton Ltd, an Hachette UK Company.

All rights reserved.

'NIV' is a registered trademark of Biblica UK trademark number 1448790.

Love's Motive

Introduction

This short book on Love has been extracted and edited from a larger one: The Who and The Why, which looks at faith, hope and love together. In that book, I argue that the most helpful way to label these three attributes, so highly valued in the bible, is as 'motivational characteristics.' That is to say, that God wants to embed these three things at the core of our souls, to both define who we are, and motivate what we do. For it's not just what we do that's important, but why we do it. God has never been looking to simply change our actions, but rather to change us from the inside out – to alter our hearts and minds so that they naturally want and pursue all that is right and good. God is constantly working in His adopted children to conform them more and more to the likeness of His Son, Jesus Christ. But this doesn't mean He's out to make us all a bunch of clones. God is far too creative for that, and besides, the infinite worth and wonder of Christ could never be captured in any single one of us. But consistent throughout each and every one of us is God's desire to embed in the core of our being a faith, hope and love, which is both sourced and sustained in God alone. These three attributes are of eternal value and will remain as relevant in the next life as they are now.

Finding love

This book tackles the greatest of these three motivational characteristics – love. But let me stress, that calling love the greatest, is not to say the others are unimportant. Both faith and hope remain vital, and to have love by itself is not enough. Indeed, as much as it's helpful to separate and understand the distinctive, different qualities of these three virtues, we must also realise that we rarely, if ever, operate out of just one of these at a time. They interact with, inform and boost each other. In turn, if one area is weak, it can hinder the others, so we must value them as a set. Nevertheless, there is one that stands out that bit brighter, love.

Tackling this subject fills me with a mix of emotions. It feels both easier and harder to write about than any other topic, and I must resign myself now to the knowledge that by the end of the book it won't feel like I've done it justice, but who truly can?

To begin we must state that it matters where our love is sourced and focused. Love is not a coverall that makes everything right. For example, the Bible contrasts a love of money vs a love of God. Other examples include being a lover of self, or lover of pleasure.[1] Equally, love cannot justify a wrong relationship and committing adultery. Love that isn't first sourced in God is going to lead you down a wrong path.

By and large, it feels that we don't need to be told how important love is – or maybe we do? Maybe because we can be so familiar with the concept, it becomes easy to brush over, not realising how devoid of love our actions can be? It was undoubtedly an issue for more than one group of people in the Bible who surely should have known better. Certainly, it seems the chief issue for both the Corinthians and the Pharisees was primarily one of the heart, not the head. Concerning the Pharisees, Jesus quoted Isaiah saying:

> *" 'These people honour me with their lips,*
>   *but their hearts are far from me.*
> *They worship me in vain;*
>   *their teachings are merely human rules.' "*
>
> Matt 15:8-9 NIV

The Pharisees were a zealous, God-fearing group, who knew the scriptures far better than most people of the time. But they completely missed the heart and character of the God behind these scriptures. So in

---

[1]. 2 Tim 3:1-4

turn, for all their knowledge, they often either miss-understood or miss-emphasised what they read and knew. Now don't be deceived, the Pharisees can be treated as a bit of a punch bag at times, and we're shown a lot of their flaws through their interactions with Jesus and His disciples. But we must always look at them as a model and warning of what we the church could so easily become should we miss the heart of God.

But also let's not swing too far the other way. Paul writing to the Philippians said: *"...it is my prayer that your love may abound more and more, with knowledge and all discernment, so that you may approve what is excellent..."*[2] Love needs knowledge and discernment to accompany it, to enable it to be truly helpful and effective. We mustn't let ourselves develop a cosy unreal sense of love being so all-important, that it doesn't matter what you do, as long as it's done in love. Many a painful deed has been done, or hurtful word been spoken with good intentions. The fact that it was motivated by love *might* soften the blow, but it doesn't stop the hit from landing.

Perhaps worse still is making the mistake that the truly awesome love of God summarises His whole character. God is far more complete and complex than that. We trivialise Him if we treat Him as just a doting father who would never punish wrong

2. Php 1:9

beyond a little word or slap on the wrist (if that). Just like us, there are many things, many motivations going on in the heart and head of God. The difference is His are all good and perfectly balanced. Whereas we're got all sorts of rubbish mixed in there, and the good we have may be unhelpfully balanced leading to bad things anyway.

Without love

Whereas the Pharisees thought of themselves as being better than others because of the rules they kept, the Corinthians thought themselves better because of the gifts they had, gifts of the Holy Spirit no less. The root issue for both these groups is that they weren't operating out of love. This fundamental issue robbed their good deeds of their potential value. Even things apparently done in God's name and for His glory were often really done to selfishly boost their own ego's and standing in their different communities. Whether it was making a show and display of the fasting they were doing,[3] or the money they were giving.[4] Or in the Corinthian's case being so desperate to share what God had told them that they wouldn't give space to others who also had something to share.[5] The human ability to take and

---

3. Matt 6:16-18
4. Matt 6:1-4
5. 1 Cor 14:29-33

do good things, then rob them of some of their worth is sadly boundless.

In addressing this issue with the Corinthian's, Paul said:

> *"... I will show you a still more excellent way.*
>
> *If I speak in the tongues of men and of angels, but have not love, I am a noisy gong or a clanging cymbal. And if I have prophetic powers, and understand all mysteries and all knowledge, and if I have all faith, so as to remove mountains, but have not love, I am nothing. If I give away all I have, and if I deliver up my body to be burned, but have not love, I gain nothing."*
>
> 1 Cor 12:31-13:3

I love this, Paul pulls no punches, and we must make sure each one of these three elements has its chance to knock some sense into us where needed.

Noise

"If I speak in the tongues of men and of angels, but have not love, I am a noisy gong or a clanging cymbal."

The human voice is a wonderful gift. With it we sing great and wonderful songs, we communicate important truths, and we can try and build each other up. But if you do any of this is without love, you're just a noise. A loud banging noise. It doesn't matter how good your singing voice is, or how good a communicator you are, without love you're just a racket in someone's ear. That's God assessment of you. But not only His, this is something we can feel towards others as well. When a person is speaking to you, whether a teacher on a platform, or someone giving you some advice face to face, if you sense it's coming out of a bad heart it's very easy to just shut down, stop listening, and they become little more than an annoying clatter going around inside your head. If we want to do others good with our voice, the first and most important act we must attend to is assessing our heart. If the motive of love isn't there, we'd do well to hold back until it is. As is often said in different ways: "unless they know that you care, they won't care what you say".

It should be noted, however, that this will be a matter of perception, and perceptions can be wrong. You might receive an encouragement or criticism given genuinely in love, worded thoughtfully and well. But instead of hearing it as intended, you immediately become offended and the barriers go up. Or maybe you yourself have said something which was taken completely in the wrong way. Whichever side of this you find yourself on you need to remember this key principle: You're responsible for your heart, not theirs.

The first step in being responsible for your own heart is testing your motives. Ask yourself why you want to challenge this person. As a rule, the majority us don't relish bringing a challenge to others, but we all need good friends who are willing, indeed loving enough to do this. And if we need others to do this for us, we certainly need to be ready and able to do it for them. As Solomon says in Proverbs: "Faithful are the wounds of a friend…"[6] Love is both the best motive and the great balancer in these situations. For those perhaps a little too willing or simply hasty in challenging others, love helps to put the brakes on and make sure due care is taken, for love is not rude. And for those more timid, love builds up the courage required to step out and do something uncomfortable but needed for their friends' sake. It is sometimes misunderstood that love would most likely just lets things pass unchallenged, and there are indeed occasions when in loving patience you should indeed just let something go. But in truth, for those of us at the timid end of things, it's frequently fear that holds us back rather than love letting something pass. Love is willing to wound if it will ultimately help. This is just another way in which love proves to be truly kind.

6. Prov 27:6

It's worth noting before moving on one other aspect of testing your own heart. Are you guilty of the same kind of mistakes? Jesus warned of judging others concerning things you also struggle with "Why do you see the speck that is in your brother's eye, but do not notice the log that is in your own eye…"[7] (Parent's - take particular note with this concerning how your talk to your children). Before you challenge someone else, take time to assess if this is something you struggle with in some way. Indeed, ask God to reveal it to you in case you're too blind to see it. He's certainly shown me a few things through such prayers. Once done, you're in a better place for talking to your friend. And even if you do have a similar issue to address, that doesn't necessarily mean you can't bring the challenge. But it will (or should) affect the way you bring it, adding that bit more humility and honesty to your conversation, for love is not proud.

With all this done, if your words are not well received, it is worth taking the time to reflect if you should have handled it differently. Again, love is not proud. If appropriate consult another trustworthy and neutral person. But if it proves all due care has been taken, take heart, and try not to let it put you off, for you were being a loving, faithful friend. Continue to pray for them, and remember, you're responsible for your heart, not theirs.

7. Matt 6:3

On the other side of this is receiving. How do you respond to challenges from others? Just as few people relish the thought of confronting others, there are probably even less who like to be confronted. It can at the very least be uncomfortable if not painful, even when said in the wisest most loving of ways. Once again, our job is to be responsible for our own heart's reaction. And love's response must be to presume the best of them, even if the challenge may have come without any perceived tact, love, or even understanding. Remember, love is not irritable or easily angered. In these circumstances, it's a good habit to go gold-digging. Search through what was said and see what nuggets of truth there may be that you can latch on to and work with to challenge yourself. On the other hand, if it has been done well, responding well is usually much easier. Love is not proud, and so it can take a wound, a faithful rebuke from caring friend, and do something good with it. Furthermore, when you find yourself on the receiving end, consider even thanking your friend for having the courage to do this. For love does not delight in evil, but rejoices with the truth. I genuinely thank God for friends that will take the trouble to faithfully wound me, and I ask for the courage to be so faithful myself.

Being Somebody

"And if I have prophetic powers, and understand all mysteries and all knowledge, and if I have all faith, so as to remove mountains, but have not love, I am nothing."

It is no doubt, not a new phenomenon at all, but it can feel like there's an even greater push these days for people to try and find both their identity and worth in all the wrong places, through all the wrong means. It might be through, sporting or business success, getting married and having children, living in the best area, having all the latest stuff, or being really important within a certain community? The church doesn't live free of this either, with any of the above creeping in to claim a value or be a driving force that they shouldn't be. Even positions of responsibility and influence within a church can be sought for all the wrong reasons. And if Paul was hard-hitting in his last charge of calling people just a noise, he's absolutely scathing now as he basically calls them a nobody! It doesn't matter how successful you've been, how wise you are, how much you know or how skilled and gifted you may be – without love, you're nothing, no one.

I hope you didn't move onto this next paragraph too quickly? Make sure you take that in because it's so easy to shake it off and not let it have its due impact. There are too many people both outside and inside the church who are seeking to be 'someone', but the way they're going about it makes them a 'no-one' in God's assessment.

Now we have another important principle to absorb: there is no direct or automatic link between gifting and character – none! Even when that gifting is a spiritual gift. It's good, essential even, to recognise God's anointing on people and to enable them to put it to good use for His glory and praise. But it's equally vital that we first also recognise good character in them before they're given authority and ministries in which to use these gifts. If the gift is there, but not the character they're not ready yet, and you must wait for both to be there before appointing people. Sadly there are some who don't see the need to grow in character first and so never get the full opportunity to step out into all that God has for them. Possibly worse still are those who *are* given the opportunity before they're ready. It's only a matter of time before this bad character will be exposed, risking God's name being tarnished in the minds of others and good works being needlessly undone. You can't of course wait for them to be perfect. That remains solely God's domain, and we're all still a work in progress. But that too I'd argue is part of the character we should be looking for – someone who's looking to grow and isn't content to stay just as they are.

Before we move on, I'd just like to acknowledge how Paul does slightly soften these blows to the Corinthian's. He doesn't actually say: "you're just a noise speaking like that", but rather: "If *I speak*… but have not love, *I am* a noisy gong…" And he doesn't say: "despite all you're your gifts, you're a nobody", but rather "…if *I have* prophetic powers, and understand all mysteries… but have not love, *I am* nothing. Paul made it initially personal to him rather than directly condemning any of them, whilst still making the point quite clear. Perhaps he's aware of how easy it would be, having the heritage that he has, and the immense Spiritual giftings, to fall for the lie that it's this that gives him his worth and makes him 'somebody'? *For love, of course, does not boast*, it does not focus on these things. Luke's gospel records when Jesus sent out in pairs seventy-two of His disciples to proclaim the Kingdom of God and heal the sick. They returned to Him jubilant saying "*Lord, even the demons are subject to us in your name!*"[8] Jesus affirms them and what had happened but also seeks to make sure they're centred correctly. He says to them: "*Nevertheless, do not rejoice in this, that the spirits are subject to you, but rejoice that your names are written in heaven*".[9] Please don't think that Jesus is being a killjoy here. He does want them to rejoice,

8. Luke 10:17
9. Luke 10:20

and acknowledge the incredible stuff that they're seeing and doing, but He wants their rejoicing centred on their standing before God, before how He's including them in His great work. In this way, He's helping to steer them away from the potential perils of becoming full of themselves, rather than full of God.

Now Paul's challenge to the Corinthian's, and in turn to us, is not to bring us down low, but to encourage us to humbly rise up in a better way. You want to be 'someone'? Brilliant! Then learn to love with zeal and humility. Train your heart in Godly loving ways, and allow it to influence and motivate you're every move. Then you will truly be a 'somebody'.

Gain

"If I give away all I have, and if I deliver up my body to be burned, but have not love, I gain nothing."

Of Paul's three quick 'punches' at the Corinthian's values, this one is surely the most surprising - I gain nothing. Following the logic of the previous two punches: without love, I'm just a loud annoying noise – but with love, I'm worth listening to; without love, I'm nothing – with love I am someone; and so now without love, I gain nothing –

but with love, I gain something. Is it right to mix the motive of love with the motive of seeking gain? Indeed, does love itself seek gain? Isn't that really selfishness instead of love? If we're treating Paul's letter to the Corinthian's as God's word (which I hope you do), then surely we must conclude that love truly does seek gain, along with seeking to speak in ways that bless and aren't just noise; and seeking to be a person of worth – truly a 'somebody' in the very best sense.

To move forwards we must address the question: how can genuine love seek gain whilst not being selfish? Consider fear for a moment. We're told many times in the Bible to fear God and the benefits of doing so.[10] But we're also told in John's first letter that "perfect love casts out fear."[11] So how do we reconcile these two things? Well, I can't claim to understand it all yet, but it would seem that there is a right and healthy way to fear God and a wrong and unhealthy way. I believe the best way to test which fear you have (if any), is to examine the effect it has on you. The unhealthy fear will leave you afraid and not wanting to be near God. A healthy fear of God will be faith born, and leave you wanting to draw closer to Him.

Similarly, there is a right and healthy way to seek gain and a wrong and unhealthy way. Let's take a very basic everyday example – food. We all want

---

10. For example: Luke 1:50; Rom 3:18; 11:20; 2 Cor 5:11 and more besides
11. 1 John 4:18; (Rom 8:15 also points to this)

to be able to eat and drink each day. Our body needs this, and to seek this 'gain' is no bad thing, we don't condemn people for this, and indeed many of us take it for granted. There is nothing in and of itself wrong about seeking gain. Selfishness, however, seeks gain at the expense, or at best in ignorance of others. It either doesn't care, or doesn't stop to think about the effect it has on other people. Concerning their practice of the Lord's Supper, Paul had to chastise the Corinthian's, even going as far as saying that it could no longer be considered a Lord's Supper because "…in eating, each one goes ahead with his own meal. One goes hungry, another gets drunk. What! Do you not have houses to eat and drink in? Or do you despise the church of God and humiliate those who have nothing?"[12] Once again, a sad example of humankind taking a good, God-given thing and utterly ruining it. And the root cause? Selfishness.

In contrast to this, we have love. And the contrast is not that love doesn't seek gain, but that it seeks gain in the benefit of others. Allow me a moment of fatherly pride here. Recently we had a little report from school concerning one of my daughters' behaviour. In it, the teacher wrote "[She] has been very busy this morning making cakes (play dough ones) for both her friends and teachers. She always finds joy in making other people feel happy." There in a nutshell, you have a great example of the

12.   1 Cor 11:22

nature of love. It seeks joy in making other people feel happy. Now some will argue that love may find joy (as if by accident) in blessing others, but would never actually seek its own joy. But I don't think that adds up with all that I find in the Bible or indeed what I experience in life. There's another name for doing things that bless others without feeling and simply for the sake of doing that thing – duty. Duty is a good and helpful thing, but we've been shown a better way – love. Love feels and seeks gain, not at the expense of others, and not as a neutral party, but in the benefit of others.

This is a really important aspect of love to grasp, so let me dwell on this for a while. If the thought of seeking your own gain turns you off as horrible thing to do, I encourage you to try reading through the Bible again whilst looking for this sort of thing, for you will find it, and not just here and there. Seeking gain in some form is a surprisingly common motivator used in the Bible. God doesn't seem to simply want our motivation to be good for goods own sake, but first for God's sake and then for our own. Because we love Him, and because we see that His way truly is the best, and the way that will bring the most gain, most joy.

Consider the most loving act of all time, Jesus Christ willingly, and purposefully died on a cross for you and me. He suffered humiliation, immense physical pain, and in ways that (praise God) those of us who believe in Him will never experience – the wrath of God over sin. Why? Because of love! And as the writer of Hebrews puts it: "…for the joy that was set before him endured the cross, despising the shame…"[13] Joy, not duty was His motivation. And what joy was this? A joy in obedience to the Father and His will, whom He loves to please. A joy in saving many souls in such a surprising and perfect way, that served justice, honoured God and made sinners righteous. For those who would go on to believe in Him, it released them to a whole new and immeasurably better life. Should that not fill Him with joy? Should He not seek His own joy through such a selfless act!?

Now let me take you to Romans:

> *"God 'will repay each person according to what they have done.' To those who by persistence in doing good seek glory, honour and immortality, he will give eternal life. But those who are self-seeking and who reject the truth and follow evil, there will be wrath and anger."*
>
> Romans 2:6-8 NIV

The good and loving actions of this first group are done seeking after glory, honour and immortality.

---

13. Heb 12:2

Does God rebuke them for a self-seeking attitude? No! He gives them exactly what they're seeking – eternal life. They're the ones genuinely living out of love. It's the next group that are accused of being self-seeking, who in turn reject the truth and follow evil.

Consider also Paul's encouragement to the Corinthian's about giving:

> *"The point is this: whoever sows sparingly will also reap sparingly, and whoever sows bountifully will also reap bountifully. Each one must give as he has decided in his heart, not reluctantly or under compulsion, for God loves a cheerful giver."*

2 Cor 9:6-7

First of all, we have a distinct appeal to the heart to do a good thing in order to gain. In this case, he's talking about giving money to others in need, though the principle can surely be applied more broadly: Sow sparingly, and you'll reap little. Sow bountifully, and you'll reap much. The picture of sowing is helpful in that it indicates an investment and patient waiting to reap the fruit (and it may be that only some or none is reaped in this life). But notice that the enticement, the motive encouraged, is to seek more gain. Furthermore giving, or doing the good deed out of a sense of obligation is positively discouraged.

God's looking for cheerful givers, not dutiful ones. Those who see the need and give out of the overflow of their heart, even if their own resources aren't overflowing.

Let's look at a different area where this is less obvious. We looked at the 'faithful wounds of a friend' earlier in the book, and we find a similar situation in parenting. Disciplining my children is no fun, not for them or me. It gives me no pleasure to do it, and them no pleasure to receive it. Yet I would not be loving my children well if I failed to do this for them. Sometimes (often) they need to be told 'no', or to face consequences for their bad behaviour. So where's the love sought gain in that? It's in the character of my ever-growing children. The love sought joy set before us as parents in these situations is one of delayed gratification. It's in the slow but ever-developing maturity of those we're responsible for, as we watch and play a key part in them growing into wonderful young men and women, so full of potential, and all being well – of good character. For in this, we know that they too will be far happier individuals if their character blossoms into something genuinely beautiful. This is something that will give me so much joy and gratitude as they reach maturity. And the cost? The cost is in our lovingly making the painful effort to train and discipline them as best we can, whilst we have both the opportunity and responsibility. So here too we find love seeking gain, in and for the benefit of others. This might also be an example of love "*always hoping*" from Paul's great description of love in 1 Corinthians, as it looks to the future good in/of others?

Finally, let me put it this way. In the end, love is about assigning true value. When we love others we're putting a worth on them in our minds, so in turn, their benefit and happiness becomes our gain too, because they've become a treasure to us.

All an Act?

What would you say love is exactly? Is it a feeling? Certainly young lovers are often counselled that there's far more to love than the excitement that abounds in the early stages of courting. Indeed love is not merely a feeling, but it rightly can have a huge effect on our emotions.

What about an action? Is love about what we do? Or on a similar note, is love a choice? Is love all about the choice to do loving acts? I've certainly been taught that before, but these verses from 1 Corinthians we've been looking at seem to tell a different story; they say that you could do incredible *acts* of love – such as giving everything you have away to the poor, for being willing to die in the flames for God's sake, and yet do them *without* love! Surely therefore love can't be described as choice or an action, because you can choose to do what might be considered incredible acts of love, but without any actual love behind it. It can prove to be just an act with ulterior motives pushing it along. This is why I believe the most helpful way to describe love (along with faith and hope), is as a motive, or rather as a motivational characteristic. God wants these (centred and sourced in Him) to define our character and motivate what we do, to be the reason we do what we do. This is why they're so important and fundamental to what God is seeking to steadily work into the core of who we are. Because it's not just important what we do, but also why we do it.

The Source

Please note that I've purposefully not tried to define love in this book. I've never found anything or been able to come up with a definition that completely satisfies me. Not even the apostle Paul seems to attempt this, instead, we get that beautiful (but not exhaustive) description of love (which we will finally get to at the end of this book). However, I am very fond of the way John Piper summed it up in his book Desiring God. "Love is the overflow of joy in God that gladly meets the needs of others".[14] Now if you were unconvinced about what I said in the last section, or simply want to consider it more, let me direct you to the book where this quote comes from and particularly his chapter on love. Once I'd processed, understood and become convinced of what he teaches in that chapter, the whole rest of the book became much easier to read and grasp. But back to the subject in hand – what I love about that quote is how rich it is in meaning, with some very choice words quickly summing up a lot of thought. The second half 'gladly meeting the needs of others', was essentially looked at in the last section. Now we take a step back to look at 'the overflow'. You cannot give what you do not have. And you cannot overflow unless you're continuously getting filled. Thankfully, as the apostle John explains, we have the greatest source of love:

> *"In this is love, not that we have loved God but that he loved us and sent his Son to be the propitiation for our sins. Beloved, if God so loved us, we also ought to love one another."*

1 John 4:10-11

This is where we must always start if we want to grow in love, not in trying harder to love God or others, but

---

14. John Piper, Desiring God, p119, 2003

in turning to both the foundation and fountain of it all – that God first loved us. He made the first move, He initiated the relationship we can now have with Him, He made that first loving step. And what an incredible step it was. He sent His Son to be the propitiation for our sins. That is to say, to be the appeasement, the offering that satisfies God on every level, and enables Him to justly release us from our debt of sin.

If you struggle to respond in love to God and others, this is where you must start. Pray and ask God to help you see and feel the immense and intense love He has for you. To help you understand just how far He came for you and the raging, heartfelt zeal behind it. Oh, God's love is tender too, patient, kind and all these wonderful things. But it is not merely nice, and it's certainly not soppy. *"For God so loved the world, that He gave His only son"*.[15] He *so* loved us that He gave that which is most precious to Him. God's love is indescribably passionate, entirely sober, and joyfully lavish. And because we have this incomprehensible Holy Trinity which is our God, we can also say that God died in our place, Jesus Christ the Son of God died for me! *"Greater love has no one than this, that someone lay down his life for his friends."*[16]

If we don't feel the depths of this, are we too familiar with the words? What's the saying?

15. John 3:16
16. John 15:13

'Familiarity breeds contempt'. I must confess that sometimes I wonder if my heart has simply become dull, dry and slow with familiarity? These great truths that my heart once leapt for joy over, are they now nothing more than head knowledge? Sadly there is probably some truth in this at times, and a bit of taking God's love for granted in an unhelpful sense. But there's something else going on too. Remember as we've already explored, love is not a feeling, it's a motive or a motivational characteristic. And so analysing whether God's love is impacting us or not is going to involve a 'what and why' type question. What do I do and why? How am I living my life in light of His love? I've been married for a good number of years now (seven when first writing this). I'll openly admit that my feelings for my wife are not felt in quite the same way as when we first started going out. My love for her is no less strong, actually I'd say its stronger. But the giddy side has diminished, and been replaced with something else, something hard to do justice in describing, but here goes – it's a more homely, comfortable feeling. There's no one I want to spend more time with, no one I feel more accepted by, no one I want to please more, and no one I feel more at home with wherever we might be. And you'll find evidence of this in my actions and decisions – making sure I get to spend regular quality time with her, and doing things I know make her happy, be it getting jobs done I'm supposed to or doing things together. Similarly with God, though He does bless me with times where it all seems so fresh and new, and I'm blown over by the love felt. But much of the time I'm operating out of a similar place to where I'm at with my wife. It's not a giddy feeling, but it is a sober passion. It remains (sadly and inevitably) meagre and woefully lacking compared to His love for me, but it is certainly there. How can we properly test this? We can't rely merely on feelings for such a test (though they remain important in different ways). I'd suggest asking yourself how you do in these three areas:

Firstly, Making time for Him. Where does God stand in your priorities from day to day? Is He someone you want to spend time with? Do you make an effort to make sure this happens? Do you miss Him, and regret it if you don't on any given day?

Secondly, Obedience. Jesus said: *"If you love me, you will keep my commandments."*[17] It's easy to forget that this is an expected result of love, we can link it more to fearing God than loving Him. Indeed, this one by itself may not be from love at all, it could be all motivated by fear or mere legalism. None of these three things by themselves are a good indicator of your love for God. All three need to be looked at together as a whole. And part of that whole that

---

17. John 14:15

you're looking for is the desire to please Him through doing what He says.

Thirdly and finally, Loving others, and in particular His people. This one, in part, flows out of the second. As Jesus said to His followers: *"This is my commandment, that you love one another as I have loved you."*[18] And then in John's first letter we read: *"If anyone says, "I love God," and hates his brother, he is a liar; for he who does not love his brother whom he has seen cannot love God whom he has not seen. And this commandment we have from him: whoever loves God must also love his brother."*[19] It is simply a natural progression or consequence that if we truly love God we will love those that He loves, we will love our brothers and sisters in Christ, who have been bought with the same blood, shed on the same cross, with whom we are now made family (hence being 'brothers and sisters'). So how do you treat your fellow Christian's? The respect, concern, and care you show for them, in both word and deed, will be a significant indicator of your love for God Himself.

> *"... if we love one another, God abides in us and his love is perfected in us."*
>
> *1 John 4:12*

---

18. John 15:12
19. 1 John 4:20-21

The Greatest

As a rule, most of the Pharisees and Scribes of Jesus time did not like Him. Some of it was jealousy as to His popularity among the people, some of it was in His actions, and much of it was because of His teaching, exposing wrong thoughts and attitudes. But there were some exceptions including one Scribe, who after witnessing several people try and trap Jesus with clever questions, instead decided to ask Him a more meaningful one.

> *"...one of the scribes came up and heard them disputing with one another, and seeing that he answered them well, asked him, "Which commandment is the most important of all?" Jesus answered, "The most important is, 'Hear, O Israel: The Lord our God, the Lord is one. And you shall love the Lord your God with all your heart and with all your soul and with all your mind and with all your strength.' The second is this: 'You shall love your neighbour as yourself.' There is no other commandment greater than these." And the scribe said to him, "You are right, Teacher. You have truly said that he is one, and there is no other besides him. And to love him with all the heart and with all the understanding and with all the strength, and to love one's neighbour as oneself, is much more than all*

whole burnt offerings and sacrifices." And when Jesus saw that he answered wisely, he said to him, "You are not far from the kingdom of God." And after that no one dared to ask him any more questions."

Mark 12:28-34

You get the impression that this Scribe's question was still a sort of test for Jesus, but one coming from a more genuine heart, more ready to accept Him if the answer was good, rather than simply trying to trap Jesus. The answer of course, was spot on, and the Scribe knew it. It's a nice place to leave this little episode. After a variety of people coming at Jesus with a bad heart and hidden motives, we end with one who may just come around to believe in Him? It should be noted also, that Jesus was not teaching a completely new thing or concept (at least it shouldn't have been new to people's ears), as He was quoting from the scriptures they already had, in particular, Deuteronomy (6:4-6) and Leviticus (19:18). Jesus didn't come and change this, He brought to light what was already there, but that had been missed by many. The two key commandments that summarise them all, and more than that, they put the right heart behind them. So, we see that love is both the greatest of the core motivators and is behind the greatest of God's commandments. We're to love

God with all our heart, soul, mind and strength. With our all. I love God, I really do, but there is no commandment that so starkly highlights to me how far short I fall. Praise God for Christ Jesus paying my debt of sin on that cross! But where do we go from here? With our debt paid, we still want to change and lead lives worthy of the calling upon them – to love God and others more and more. How do we change and grow? We've already looked at the source of our love, and resting in God's love for us must always be the first step if we're to start right with the best foundations. Thankfully our help doesn't stop there either, as the Holy Spirit now works in us to change us from within, and love is the first of the fruit, the first evidence of His growing in us listed in Galatians.[20] But still, what can we do?

> *"For those who live according to the flesh set their minds on the things of the flesh, but those who live according to the Spirit set their minds on the things of the Spirit."*
>
> *Romans 8:5*

Now don't think of your mind as being your purely logical side. Trust me, you and your mind are not fully logical. But we do have a control over our minds that we don't have with our desires or emotions. We all have a mixture of desires going on inside us, some

---

20. Gal 5:22

good, some bad, and all sorts of emotions going on alongside this. The question is what are you going to do with them? What's required of us is to set our minds (the element we do control) on the things of the Spirit – on what He desires, on what is good and right and Godly. And in so doing this we start to train our desires, feeding the good and hopefully starving the bad. Here we find an ongoing principle in the Bible. If you want to change, don't just try to cut out the bad, but also replace it with something good. So here it's both taking our minds off wrong and ungodly desires, and putting them on what the Spirit desires, on what is good. So for example, if you struggle with gossip and have a habit of slandering people behind their back, don't just try and stop doing that, but make a conscious decision and effort to speak well of people and build them up. Not just when they're not around, but encourage them to their face. In this way, you'll start to change from being someone who tears down in secret, to someone who builds up in public. You've moved from setting your mind on things that the 'flesh' so often craves, to things that the Holy Spirit within you desires. You've got behind and worked alongside the Spirit, and so, in turn, have become a more loving person.

How to grow old

Let me share with you in good length, one of my favourite stories of someone who embodied a life of love and was still growing in this as she got ever older. Evelyn was born in England in 1879, the ninth of eleven children. From early on is was evident that she had a very independent character, with a love of colours, painting and all living things. At the age of thirty, Evelyn announced to her family that God had called her to become a missionary to India. Her dad, not wanting her to go, insisted that she get checked out by a doctor first, to make sure she'd be physically capable of living in the tropics without harm to her health. She passed with flying colours. Evelyn was not the flimsy petal her beautiful and fashionable dresses could make her seem. She was made of tougher stuff, and her dad relented, having to concede that she must follow God's will above his own.

Assigned to the Madras region of India, she went about her training, learning languages and some medical skills among other things. Here she met the same young man, Jesse Brand, whose talk God had used to call her to the mission field. They soon found they were of a kindred spirit, and together embarked on a mission to bring the gospel to a region of five mountain ranges that had become known as the 'Mountains of Death'.[21] They were married in sight

---

21. A collection of five mountain ranges; the Kollis (where they started), Pachais, Kalrayan, Peria Malai, and Chitteris

of the Kolli mountain range, and the very next day set off together for their new home, which Jesse had built up on the hill ready for them. They spent their time teaching better farming methods, treating the sick, helping build houses for the poorest, and of course teaching the people there about God. Except for one death bed conversion early on, they went seven years without seeing anyone saved. Seven years of what might feel like failure, but they persisted in love and faith. The turning point came when a Hindu priest who carried great influence and who had been adamantly against them caught the fever. Jesse and Evelyn hurried to his aid. As he died, the priest entrusted his children to the Brands. 'The Jesus God must be the true one', he said, because the Brands alone had helped him in his hour of death.

Jesse and Evelyn continued together for another thirteen years of slow but productive ministry, helping many people, and started to see more and more people saved, before Jesse himself succumbed to Blackwater Fever. Evelyn was devastated, and everyone it seemed, expected her to go back home at this point. But that was not on her mind. She felt God wanted her to complete the task she and her husband had started. Now at fifty years old, she spends the next twenty continuing to work for the mission in India on the Kolli hills. At sixty-nine, she sought to start a new work in the Kalryans, but was denied by the missions board, because she was old, single, and possibly because she was so stubbornly opinionated. She'd given the mission board trouble on several occasions, and they weren't for budging on this. Evelyn clutched at one last straw. 'Please just send me back for one last year,' she pleaded. 'I promise not to make any more trouble.' The board relented, and in this final year with the help of her two children, she smuggled in materials and had a little bungalow built for herself in the mountains. Her final year with the mission ended; fellow missionaries gathered to wish her a tearful good-bye. But Evelyn told them gleefully that she wasn't going home.

Instead, she bought a pony and started travelling from village to village in the Kalryans, sharing the gospel and loving people in whatever way she could. Finally, she'd been able to start bringing the gospel to the second of five mountain ranges that she and Jesse had always dreamed of reaching.

She spent another twenty-three years travelling from village to village loving people, becoming known as Granny Brand. Broken bones, sickness, ageing, her battles with the marijuana growers... it seemed nothing would stop her. With the help of a growing group of people, she brought the message of the gospel to the five mountain ranges, and a further two beyond.[22] At the age of ninety she was on a trip back to the Kollis, and the place where it all started

22. The Bothais and Paithur hills

for her. This time she had her niece, Dr Ruth, for company. To Evelyn's surprise, her memories of the place were no longer marred with bitterness towards the mission board, which from her point of view, had both neglected and compromised the work which she and Jesse had started. The matter had simply become unimportant to her anymore. Her son Paul had noticed this change in her just a few months prior. In a letter, he wrote that he'd found her "distinctly younger than she was a year ago." At first, this puzzled him as she was not physically any stronger. But then 'he put his finger on it' – for many years her love for these hill people had been contending within her with an anger towards those she felt had hindered the work. Now it seemed her love had been able to extend further still to include those who had unintentionally, perhaps not been so helpful in the work being done there? The result was a peace and inner strength that made her shine all the more. "This is how to grow old," Paul had written, "Allow everything else to fall away, until those around you see just love. They will also see your own life renewed and they will recognise the love, to be the love of God."

At ninety-three years old she was still going, still pushing with what strength remained in her frail body to care for others and share the wonderful story of Jesus Christ. Becoming too unbalanced to ride a donkey anymore, men from the surrounding villages came and put her in a hammock and carried her from village to village because they loved her so much. Through this, she was enabled to keep teaching and telling the story of her beloved Jesus for another two years. Two years more lived and given as a gift of love, carried in a hammock, doing whatever she still could to help the poorest of the poor. She continued this work nearly to her very dying day, when the Lord finally brought His good and faithful servant home.[23]

Record keeping

I love the story of Evelyn 'Granny' Brand, and have often been struck by a quote from her son describing this beloved character. "This is how to grow old…" And finally reading a fuller account of her story put this quote of his into its proper context for me. This wonderfully loving lady just kept growing in character, and now it seemed she had learned to forgive those she had viewed as obstructing, or at the very least being unhelpful to the work she and her late husband had started. The result was a new youthfulness added to this ninety-year-old. If I live to be that old, I dearly want to be someone who is still growing in character and wisdom with God. Oh, what needless weight we carry, when we

---

23. For a fuller account of Evelyn's story, I can recommend: Dorothy Clarke Wilson, Granny Brand Her Story, 1976

fail to forgive. It seems that it does more harm to us than to those we hold the grudge against. *Love keeps no record of wrongs* we're told. Yet in this, I do wonder if we sometimes teach this slightly wrong and take it a little too far. What I mean is, we read something like: "*For I will be merciful toward their iniquities, and I will remember their sins no more.*"[24] And take it to mean that God literally forgets our sin. Like He gives Himself amnesia just in this precise area. Then you get teaching that encourages you by saying: "You don't need to say to God sorry for sinning in this way yet *again*, because He literally can't remember the last time after He forgave you." Forgive and forget? But is that truly the dynamic going on between us and God? My impression (and of course I could be wrong – impressions/feelings do not trump the authority of scripture), is that as I interact with God and bring to Him my confessions, He isn't oblivious to the fact that I have ongoing issues, or that He's had to forgive me about this before. He hasn't forgotten, but He has forgiven and does not *count* them against me.

Let me try and illustrate this in another way. I was horrified with myself one morning when I realised that when I saw one of my daughters for the first time that day, I was not looking at them with the eyes of fatherly love but with condemnation. Her behaviour the previous evening had, let's just say, not

---

24. Heb 8:12

been good. I had not yet forgiven her, and my mercies were not new that morning like God's were. I had kept a record in my head and heart. Quickly and internally I turned to God, asking Him to forgive my unforgiveness, my petty grudge against my own beautiful daughter! Furthermore, I asked the Spirit to help me properly forgive her, in which He was quick and eager to oblige. Now my role as a father means that I have a key part to play in helping my children grow up into people of good character. To do this well, I need to be aware of where they struggle, to be able to see the difference between patterns of behaviour and blips along the way. If I literally forget what they've done I can't do this, and so I cannot help them so well. What I need is not to forget, but to not keep a record. There's a subtle yet substantial difference here. In not keeping record I'm not keeping it against them, I'm not there ready to bring back their whole past upon them, and perhaps most importantly, when I look at them, I'm not seeing their flaws, but the wonderfully and fearfully God-made person that He has graciously put in my life. A person He's put there for me to love, cherish, and ultimately release into the world with all the potential they have within. It's all about how we view people. Do we just see the flaws and let that define our image of them? Or do we see the person with eyes of love, valuing them? Not holding a record of past sins against them, but neither being blind and silly, pretending that they're perfect as they are.

When my loving Heavenly Father looks at me, I know that He does not see all my sins heaped up against me, for He has truly removed them as far as the east is from the west.[25] But neither is He under any illusions as to my current condition. I'm growing and getting better by His Holy Spirit at work in me, and one day, when He brings this life to a close and gives me a new body, I will finally be made perfect and totally free from sin in every sense. Maybe its at that point when the work is complete, He will truly remember my sins no more? Until that day He knowingly, and patiently continues His good work of transformation in me. Praise God.

A good ambition

I've purposefully not delved into Paul's beautiful description of love found in 1 Corinthians. It just never seemed like the right thing to do for this book, but I hope you noted the semi-frequent references to it. Now as we draw to a close, I encourage you to read Paul's words anew, delight in them, cherish them. Then make it your ambition, through the work of the Holy Spirit, to make these words a more and more accurate description of you

25. Psalm 103:12

with each year of life that passes. Indeed, letting all else fall away till all that remains is love. For...

> *"Love is patient, love is kind. It does not envy, it does not boast, it is not proud. It does not dishonour others, it is not self-seeking, it is not easily angered, it keeps no record of wrongs. Love does not delight in evil, but rejoices with the truth. It always protects, always trusts, always hopes, and always perseveres."*
>
> 1 Corinthians 13:4-7 NIV

Other books in this series:

Faith's Motive:

Faith goes beyond mere belief, even demons know about the one true God. Faith runs deeper and takes you further, constantly affirming to your soul – God is Greater!

Faith is the foundation of these.

Other books in this series:

Hope's Motive:

Often used merely to describe our wishes or optimism; other times expressed in ways that make it indistinguishable from faith. But hope has its own unique and vital function, raising our sight and bringing God centred anticipation.

Hope is the lifter of these.

www.ingramcontent.com/pod-product-compliance
Lightning Source LLC
Chambersburg PA
CBHW071546080526
44588CB00011B/1815